Syllables and Affixes, Volume 1

Words Their Way
CLASSROOM

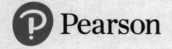

Pearson

Glenview, Illinois   Boston, Massachusetts
Chandler, Arizona   New York, New York

Photographs

Cover Anneka/Shutterstock; ARTIKAL/Shutterstock; Janis Abolins/Shutterstock; Mathee Suwannarak/Shutterstock; Perunika/Shutterstock

Pearson Education, Inc. 330 Hudson Street, New York, NY 10013

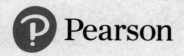

ISBN 13: 978-1-4284-4191-0
ISBN-10:   1-4284-4191-3

6   19

Contents

CVVC	CVC	CVCC	CVCe
chief	wrap	smell	whine
brief	twig	when	brave
plot	scout	groan	thank
fruit	theme	stain	clog
quit	phone	quote	front
climb	trust	sharp	scale

Review of Vowel Patterns in One-Syllable Words

CVVC	CVC	CVCC	CVCe
chief	wrap	smell	whine

Sort 1: Review of Vowel Patterns in One-Syllable Words   3

Read each of the words in the box. Write each word in the correct column.

fruit	brief	twig	when	brave	plot	scout	groan
thank	theme	stain	clog	quit	phone	quote	front
climb	trust	sharp	scale				

CVVC
chief

CVC
wrap

CVCC
smell

CVCe
whine

rest	yell	run	swim
standing	jump	sit	passing
pick	put	yelling	swimming
putting	pass	stand	running
picking	jumping	resting	sitting

+ -ing	VCC base word	double + -ing	VC base word
asking	ask	getting	get

Complete each sentence by adding the ending -ing to the word in parentheses. Write the word on the line.

My neighbor is _____ flowers from his garden. (pick)

Rosa is _____ in a race this weekend. (run)

My mother and I like _____ together on the sofa. (rest)

Luke is _____ the ball to his teammate. (pass)

Jamal likes _____ on the park bench. (sit)

Kyle thinks _____ rope is fun. (jump)

The librarian is _____ away the returned books. (put)

Ling enjoys _____ each day after school. (swim)

Our teacher doesn't like _____ in the classroom. (yell)

Pablo gets bored _____ around. (stand)

The weather is _____ better. (get)

Sarah can't go without first _____ her parents. (ask)

VCe base word	e-drop + -ing	VVC base word	+ -ing
ice	icing	sneak	sneaking
blame	score	tune	eating
use	clean	rain	ride
raining	driving	load	drive
cleaning	blaming	read	using
scoring	riding	eat	loading
tuning	reading		

+ -ing						
sneaking						

VVC base word						
sneak						

e-drop + -ing						
icing						

VCe base word						
ice						

Make new words by adding the ending -ing to the following base words. Write the new words on the lines. Then write a sentence containing each new word.

blame _____

clean _____

score _____

rain _____

use _____

tune _____

ride _____

load _____

drive _____

read _____

eat _____

ice _____

double + -ed	e-drop + -ed	+ -ed
stopped	**smiled**	**fished**
rocked	roared	traded
wagged	graded	clipped
baked	stamped	named
closed	sailed	knitted
farmed	started	knotted
scored	rubbed	scarred
stared	handed	waved
skated	marked	whizzed

Adding -ed (Double/e-Drop/No Change)

double + -ed	e-drop + -ed	+ -ed
stopped	**smiled**	**fished**

Make new words by adding the ending -ed to the base words. Write the new words on the lines. Then write a sentence containing each new word.

roar _____

bake _____

start _____

stop _____

grade _____

farm _____

fish _____

clip _____

smile _____

knot _____

wave _____

hand _____

Sort 4: Adding -ed (Double/e-Drop/No Change)

keep	shone
threw	freeze
slide	kept
froze	drive
bleed	slid
drew	sweep
know	drove
bled	draw
shine	knew
swept	throw

present	past
sleep	**slept**

Write the irregular past-tense form of each verb on the line. Then write a sentence containing the past-tense verb.

sleep _____

keep _____

draw _____

shine _____

sweep _____

throw _____

know _____

freeze _____

drive _____

slide _____

bleed _____

Sort 5: Unusual Past-Tense Words

Plural Endings -es, -s

add -s	add -es -s messes	add -es -x foxes	add -es -sh brushes	add -es -ch benches
gloves	speeches	wishes	buses	taxes
splashes	churches	mixes	horses	scratches
crashes	kisses	classes	peaches	voices
lunches	places	branches	changes	leashes
ashes				

Plural Endings -es, -s

Sort each of the following 16 words into a column. Read the words and columns.

add -es -ch benches	add -es -sh brushes	add -es -x foxes	add -es -s messes	add -s gloves

Sort 6: Plural Endings -es, -s

23

Make each of the following singular words plural by adding -s or -es. Write the words on the lines.

singular	plural	singular	plural
wish	_____	place	_____
kiss	_____	splash	_____
voice	_____	lunch	_____
speech	_____	change	_____
class	_____	crash	_____
bus	_____	branch	_____
scratch	_____	mix	_____
horse	_____	ash	_____
peach	_____	church	_____
tax	_____	leash	_____

Unusual Plurals

goose	knife	life	leaf
knives	mouse	women	deer
mice	geese	teeth	wolves
leaves	tooth	woman	loaf
wolf	sheep	loaves	lives

Unusual Plurals

no change	vowel change		-f or -fe to -ves	
	feet	foot	wives	wife

Underline the word in each sentence that means more than one. Then write the singular form of the word on the line.

Devon thinks his cat will have nine lives. _____

Look at the geese flying through the air. _____

The kitchen knives are kept on the counter. _____

Ella often sees deer in her backyard. _____

Mia makes loaves of bread each week. _____

There were mice on the farm. _____

At night I hear wolves howling. _____

There are many women at the store. _____

Raj petted the sheep at the zoo. _____

My mother brushes her teeth after she eats. _____

The restaurant had a party for the wives. _____

Lily dipped her feet in the pool. _____

+ -ing	+ -s	+ -ed
crying	**cries**	**cried**
replying	copying	carrying
studying	stays	hurried
replied	enjoying	copied
studies	replies	carries
enjoys	stayed	hurries
staying	studied	copies
carried	enjoyed	hurrying

+ -ing	+ -s	+ -ed
crying	cries	cried

Read each word. Make new words by adding the endings -ing, -s or -es, and -ed. (Change y to i as necessary.) Write the new words in the correct columns.

	-ing	-s or + -es	-ed
reply			
copy			
enjoy			
hurry			
stay			
study			
carry			
cry			

bookmark	snowflake	downstairs	headfirst	lightweight
headlight	daylight	snowstorm	bookworm	downtown
cookbook	downpour	headphones	flashlight	snowplow
countdown	scrapbook	snowball	headstrong	sunlight

Compound Words

bookcase	lighthouse	downhill	headline	snowman

Choose words from the box to make new words. On the lines, write the two words that make up the compound word and the compound word itself. You may use each word more than once.

book	case	cook	count	day	down	first	flake	flash	head	light
mark	phones	plow	snow	stairs	storm	strong	sun	town	weight	pour

_____ + _____ = _____

_____ + _____ = _____

_____ + _____ = _____

_____ + _____ = _____

_____ + _____ = _____

_____ + _____ = _____

_____ + _____ = _____

_____ + _____ = _____

_____ + _____ = _____

_____ + _____ = _____

_____ + _____ = _____

_____ + _____ = _____

_____ + _____ = _____

_____ + _____ = _____

_____ + _____ = _____

_____ + _____ = _____

More Compound Words

backpack	homework	driveway	lifeboat	earache
homesick	lifetime	earring	background	backfire
hallway	stairway	lifeguard	backbone	earplug
backyard	homemade	lifelong	wayside	homestretch
backtrack	doorway	hometown	eardrum	

earache	lifeboat	driveway	homework	backpack

Sort 10: More Compound Words (39)

Choose words from the box to make new words. On the lines, write the two words that make up the compound word and the compound word itself.
You may use each word more than once.

back	way	pack	life	yard	ground	guard	long	ear	bone
sick	drum	work	fire	home	made	ring	ache	boat	stretch
plug	town	track	drive	hall	stair	side	door	time	

_____ + _____ = _____

_____ + _____ = _____

_____ + _____ = _____

_____ + _____ = _____

_____ + _____ = _____

_____ + _____ = _____

_____ + _____ = _____

_____ + _____ = _____

_____ + _____ = _____

_____ + _____ = _____

_____ + _____ = _____

_____ + _____ = _____

_____ + _____ = _____

_____ + _____ = _____

_____ + _____ = _____

_____ + _____ = _____

Abstract Compound Words

inside	without	everything	himself	somebody
nothing	sometime	outfit	somehow	anything
herself	myself	somewhere	themselves	beside
sideways	itself	outside	yourself	someone
	something	throughout	outfield	checkout

inside	without	everything	himself	somebody

Choose words from the box to make new words. On the lines, write the two words that make up the compound word and the compound word itself. You may use each word more than once.

any	them	selves	some	thing	be	your	through	no	one	out	side	time
her	check	in	my	self	ways	how	where	it	body	him	every	with

_____ + _____ = _____

_____ + _____ = _____

_____ + _____ = _____

_____ + _____ = _____

_____ + _____ = _____

_____ + _____ = _____

_____ + _____ = _____

_____ + _____ = _____

_____ + _____ = _____

_____ + _____ = _____

_____ + _____ = _____

_____ + _____ = _____

_____ + _____ = _____

_____ + _____ = _____

_____ + _____ = _____

_____ + _____ = _____

dinner	pretty	diner
tiger	penny	later
paper	puppy	rabbit
even	over	kitten
hello	ruler	lesson
busy	crazy	summer
open	happy	tiny

Syllable Juncture in VCV and VCCV Patterns

-VCV- super	-VCCV- supper	Oddball

Read each of the words in the box. Write the words in the correct column. Break the words into two syllables by drawing a line between the two syllables.

dinner	pretty	diner	tiger	penny	later
paper	rabbit	even	over	kitten	hello
lesson	busy	crazy	summer	open	happy

-VCV-	-VCCV-	Oddball
su/per	sup/per	
_____	_____	_____
_____	_____	_____
_____	_____	_____
_____	_____	_____
_____	_____	_____
_____	_____	_____
_____	_____	_____
_____	_____	_____

Sort 12: Syllable Juncture in VCV and VCCV Patterns

Syllable Juncture in VCV and VVCV Patterns

never	pilot	trainer	river
student	peanut	planet	frozen
seven	humor	finish	leader
second	sneaker	visit	lazy
lemon	music	minute	easy

Sort 13: Syllable Juncture in VCV and VVCV Patterns

Syllable Juncture in VCV and VVCV Patterns

-V/CV- long	-VC/V- short	-VVCV- long
human	**wagon**	**reason**

Read each of the words in the box. Write the words in the correct column. Break the words into two syllables by drawing a line between the two syllables.

river	seven	never	sneaker	peanut	minute	finish
humor	pilot	visit	planet	easy	leader	lemon
trainer	lazy	frozen	second	student	music	

-V/CV- long	-VC/V- short	-VVCV- long
hu/man	wag/on	rea/son
_____	_____	_____
_____	_____	_____
_____	_____	_____
_____	_____	_____
_____	_____	_____
_____	_____	_____
_____	_____	_____
_____	_____	_____

riot	kingdom	complete	poet
subtract	monster	dial	pumpkin
cruel	sandwich	trial	address
hundred	lion	control	mushroom
children	giant	inspect	diet

Syllable Juncture in VCCCV and VV Patterns

-VCC/CV-	-VC/CCV-	-V/V-
athlete	pilgrim	create

Read each of the words in the box. Write the words in the correct column. Break the words into two syllables by drawing a line between the two syllables.

poet	complete	riot	kingdom	pumpkin	subtract	monster
dial	address	trial	sandwich	cruel	mushroom	control
lion	hundred	diet	inspect	giant	children	

-VCC/CV-	-VC/CCV-	-V/V-
ath/lete	pil/grim	cre/ate
_____	_____	_____
_____	_____	_____
_____	_____	_____
_____	_____	_____
_____	_____	_____
_____	_____	_____
_____	_____	_____

Sort 14: Syllable Juncture in VCCCV and VV Patterns

plotting	meeting	quoted
waited	faded	spelling
writing	nodded	shouting
acted	floated	skated
wanted	saving	standing
needed	hunted	taking
getting	using	leaking

Open and Closed Syllables and Inflected Endings

-VCV-	-VCCV-	-VVCV-
hoping	**hopping**	**cleaning**

Read each of the words in the box. Write the words in the correct column. Break the words into two syllables by drawing a line between the two syllables.

plotting	meeting	quoted	waited	faded	spelling	writing
nodded	shouting	acted	floated	skated	wanted	saving
standing	needed	hunted	taking	getting	using	leaking

-VCV-	-VCCV-	-VVCV-
hop/ing	hop/ping	clean/ing
_____	_____	_____
_____	_____	_____
_____	_____	_____
_____	_____	_____
_____	_____	_____
_____	_____	_____
_____	_____	_____

Sort 15: Open and Closed Syllables and Inflected Endings

complain	painter	decay
mistake	crayon	parade
private	mayor	maybe
escape	bracelet	amaze
pavement	basement	explain
railroad	raisin	today
remain	payment	obey

Long a Patterns in Accented Syllables

ā in 1st Syllable	ā in 2nd Syllable	Oddball
rainbow	**awake**	

Read each of the long a words in the box. Write the words in the column that shows the vowel pattern they contain. Draw a line between the two syllables. Then underline the accented syllable.

complain	painter	decay	mistake	crayon
parade	railroad	mayor	maybe	escape
bracelet	amaze	pavement	basement	explain

$\overline{ai}$	$\overline{a}\_e$	$\overline{ay}$
rain/bow	a/wake	pay/ment
_____	_____	_____
_____	_____	_____
_____	_____	_____
_____	_____	_____
_____	_____	_____
_____	_____	_____
_____	_____	_____

delight	ninety	surprise
machine	decide	higher
advice	brightly	survive
forgive	driveway	combine
slightly	arrive	lightning
provide	sidewalk	favorite
invite	highway	describe

Long i Patterns in Accented Syllables

ī in 1st syllable		ī in 2nd syllable		Oddball
frighten		**polite**		

Read each of the long i words in the box. Write the words in the column that shows the vowel pattern they contain. Draw a line between the two syllables. Then underline the accented syllable.

delight	ninety	surprise	machine	decide	higher	advice
brightly	survive	forgive	driveway	combine	slightly	arrive
lightning	provide	favorite	highway			

īgh	ī_e	Oddball
fright/en	po/lite	
_____	_____	_____
_____	_____	_____
_____	_____	_____
_____	_____	_____
_____	_____	_____
_____	_____	_____
_____	_____	_____
_____	_____	_____

explode	pony	suppose
lonely	compose	owner
bureau	lower	decode
lonesome	remote	loafer
alone	closely	Europe
soapy	approach	robot
awoke	sofa	erode

Oddball

ō in 2ⁿᵈ syllable

below

ō in 1ˢᵗ syllable

toaster

Read each of the long *o* words in the box. Write the words in the column that shows the vowel pattern they contain. Draw a line between the two syllables. Then underline the accented syllable.

suppose	lonely	compose	owner	closely
decode	lower	remote	loafer	alone
erode	soapy	approach	awoke	

o̅a	o̅_e	o̅CC or o̅w
toas/ter	ex/plode	be/low
_____	_____	_____
_____	_____	_____
_____	_____	_____
_____	_____	_____
_____	_____	_____
_____	_____	_____
_____	_____	_____
_____	_____	_____

Sort 18: Long o Patterns in Accented Syllables

Long u Patterns oo and u_e in Accented Syllables

ū in 1st syllable	ū in 2nd syllable	Oddball
rooster	**include**	
reduce	balloon	useful
cartoon	doodle	Tuesday
moody	refuse	raccoon
toothache	excuse	noodle
beauty	shampoo	pollute
conclude	scooter	confuse
cocoon	cougar	amuse

Long u Patterns oo and u_e in Accented Syllables

ū in 1st syllable	ū in 2nd syllable	Oddball
rooster	**include**	

Sort 19: Long u Patterns oo and u_e in Accented Syllables (75)

Read each of the long u words in the box. Write the words in the column that shows the vowel pattern they contain. Draw a line between the two syllables. Then underline the accented syllable.

amuse	Tuesday	raccoon	useful	pollute	moody
confuse	doodle	reduce	toothache	balloon	scooter
shampoo	beauty	cartoon	cougar	conclude	noodle

o͞o	u̅_e	Oddball
roos/ter	in/clude	
_____	_____	_____
_____	_____	_____
_____	_____	_____
_____	_____	_____
_____	_____	_____
_____	_____	_____
_____	_____	_____
_____	_____	_____

Sort 19: Long u Patterns oo and u_e in Accented Syllables

ē in 1st syllable	ĕ in 1st syllable	ē in 2nd syllable
needle	**feather**	**succeed**
leather	increase	season
compete	reader	heavy
defeat	pleasant	feature
sweater	freedom	indeed
meaning	steady	extreme
fifteen	eastern	repeat
thirteen	healthy	

ē in 1st syllable	ĕ in 1st syllable	ē in 2nd syllable
needle	**feather**	**succeed**

Read each of the words in the box. Write the words in the column that shows the vowel pattern and sound they contain. Draw a line between the two syllables. Then underline the accented syllable.

leather	increase	sweater	compete	reader	heavy	defeat
pleasant	feature	freedom	indeed	meaning	steady	thirteen
extreme	fifteen	eastern	repeat	healthy		

ēe or ē_e	ĕa	ēa
nee/dle	feath/er	sea/son
_____	_____	_____
_____	_____	_____
_____	_____	_____
_____	_____	_____
_____	_____	_____
_____	_____	_____
_____	_____	_____

lightning	useful	invade
debate	speaker	freezer
delete	disease	flowing
crayon	define	advice
compose	decay	refrain
remote	enclose	frighten
salute	dispute	dainty
awake	polite	brightly

Review Long Vowel Patterns in Accented Syllables

Long Vowel in 2nd Syllable

Long Vowel in 1st Syllable

1. Read each phrase. Look at the word in boldface type. Draw a line between the two syllables.
2. Circle the long vowel in each boldface word.
3. Underline the accented syllable of each boldface word.

colored **crayon**	**define** the word
invade with caution	close the **freezer**
seek **advice**	shining **brightly**
delete the mistakes	**debate** the issue
don't **frighten** animals	**useful** instructions
salute the officer	**lightning** bolt
flowing river	**remote** control
chronic **disease**	guest **speaker**
dispute the charges	**enclose** the yard
use **polite** manners	sing the **refrain**
dainty flowers	**compose** a story

Sort 21: Review Long Vowel Patterns in Accented Syllables

Ambiguous Vowels oy/oi and ou/ow in Accented Syllables

1st Syllable		2nd Syllable		Oddball
oi/oy	**ou/ow**	**oi/oy**	**ou/ow**	
voyage	drowsy	country	destroy	announce
moisture	coward	amount	thousand	avoid
poison	trouble	noisy	annoy	employ
allow	double	loyal	county	around
about	appoint	counter	southern	pointed

Ambiguous Vowels **oy/oi** and **ou/ow** in Accented Syllables

1st Syllable

oi/oy	ou/ow

2nd Syllable

oi/oy	ou/ow	Oddball

Sort 22: Ambiguous Vowels oy/oi and ou/ow in Accented Syllables (87)

1. Write on the lines words that contain vowel patterns oy, oi, ou, and ow.
2. Circle the vowel pair within the word.
3. Choose two words and use each in a sentence. Write your sentences on the lines below.

oy **voyage**	oi **moisture**	ow **drowsy**

ou **announce**	ou **country**

1. _____

_____

2. _____

_____

au saucer	aw awful	al also	oddball
always	author	salty	August
all right	lawyer	walnut	awkward
autumn	laundry	laughed	awesome
gnawing	caution	flawless	faucet
alter	auction	gawking	sausage
haunted			

Ambiguous Vowels au/aw/al in Accented Syllables

au	aw	al	Oddball
saucer	awful	also	

1. Read each of the words in the box. Write the words in the column that shows the vowel pattern they contain.

2. Draw a line between the two syllables in each word. Underline the accented syllable of each word.

3. Choose three words and use each in a sentence. Write your sentences on the lines below.

awkward	laundry	always	gnawing	haunted	walnut
lawyer	gawking	alter	faucet	caution	flawless
autumn	sausage	awesome	author	salty	

au	aw	al
<u>sau</u>/cer	<u>aw</u>/ful	<u>al</u>/so

1. _____

2. _____

3. _____

r-Influenced a in Accented Syllables

ar in 1st Syllable	ā in 1st Syllable	ā in 2nd Syllable	Oddball
garden	airplane	compare	
careful	beware	fairy	harvest
carpet	barely	partner	barefoot
haircut	aware	toward	declare
repair	parents	market	pardon
hardly	marble	despair	dairy

r-Influenced a in Accented Syllables

ar in 1st Syllable	ā in 1st Syllable	ā in 2nd Syllable	Oddball
garden	airplane	compare	

Sort 24: r-Influenced a in Accented Syllables (95)

1. Write on the lines words that contain the r-influenced a in the first syllable or the second syllable.
2. Choose three words and use each in a sentence. Write your sentences on the lines below.

ar in 1st Syllable	ā in 1st Syllable	ā in 2nd Syllable
garden	airplane	compare

1. _____

2. _____

3. _____

Sort 24: r-Influenced a in Accented Syllables

or in 1st Syllable	or in 2nd Syllable	Oddball
morning	**report**	
order	record	shorter
perform	forest	sorry
normal	reward	corner
ashore	forty	before
northern	explore	border
forward	corncob	chorus
ignore	adore	florist
inform		

r-Influenced o in Accented Syllables

or in 1st Syllable									or in 2nd Syllable									Oddball							
morning									report																

Sort 25: r-Influenced o in Accented Syllables

1. Write on the lines words that contain the r-influenced o in the first syllable or the second syllable.
2. Choose three words and use each in a sentence. Write your sentences on the lines below.

or in 1st Syllable	or in 2nd Syllable	Oddball
morning	report	

1. _____

   _____

2. _____

   _____

3. _____

   _____

Sort 25: r-Influenced o in Accented Syllables

wardrobe	worse	waffle
warning	world	wander
warden	worry	squat
warrior	worthy	squash
quarter	worship	squabble
quarrel	worthwhile	squad
swarm	dwarf	backward

war	wor	wa
warmth	worker	watch

1. Write on the lines words that contain w or the /w/ sound before the vowel.
2. Choose three words and use each in a sentence. Write your sentences on the lines below.

war	wor	wa
warmth	worker	watch

1. _____

_____

2. _____

_____

3. _____

_____

Sort 27

r-Influenced er, ir, ur in First Syllables

er	ir	ur	Oddball
nervous	**thirty**	**sturdy**	
person	firmly	purpose	furnish
spirit	perfect	dirty	service
further	every	certain	during
birthday	furry	mermaid	Thursday
thirsty	turtle	perhaps	circle
birdbath			

Sort 27: r-Influenced er, ir, ur in First Syllables

r-Influenced er, ir, ur in First Syllables

er	ir	ur	Oddball
nervous	**thirty**	**sturdy**	

1. Write words that contain er, ir, and ur in the first syllable.
2. Choose three words and use each in a sentence. Write your sentences on the lines below.

er	ir	ur
nervous	thirty	sturdy

1. _____

_____

2. _____

_____

3. _____

_____

r-Influenced Vowels er, ear, ere, eer in Accented Syllables

ėr		r-Influenced ē		
er = /ur/	ear = /ur/	ear	ere	eer
mercy	early	nearby	severe	career
sermon	earthquake	teardrop	thermos	rehearse
sincere	cheerful	serpent	appear	kernel
learner	spearmint	adhere	yearning	dreary
hermit	pearly	yearbook	earnest	searching
merely				

Sort 28: r-Influenced Vowels er, ear, ere, eer in Accented Syllables (109)

r-Influenced Vowels **er, ear, ere, eer** in Accented Syllables

ėr		
er = /ur/	**ear = /ur/**	
mercy	early	

r-Influenced ē

ear	**ere**	**eer**
nearby	severe	career

Copyright © Pearson Education, Inc., or its affiliates. All Rights Reserved.

1. Write words that contain r-influenced vowels on the lines.
2. Choose two words and use each in a sentence. Write your sentences on the lines below.

ėr	
er = /ur/	**ear = /ur/**
<u>mer</u>/cy	<u>ear</u>/ly

r-Influenced ē		
ear	**ere**	**eer**
<u>near</u>/by	se/<u>vere</u>	ca/<u>reer</u>

1. _____

_____

2. _____

_____

Sort 28: r-Influenced Vowels er, ear, ere, eer in Accented Syllables